THE ULTIMATE SOURCE

FOR **YOUR** NEEDS

RICHARD ROBERTS

Unless otherwise noted, scripture quotations are taken from the New King James Version® Copyright © 1982 by Thomas Nelson. Used by permission. All rights reserved.

Scripture quotations marked AMP are from the Amplified Version, copyright © 1954, 1958, 1962, 1964, 1965, 1987, 2015 by Zondervan and The Lockman Foundation. Used by permission.

Scripture quotations marked MSG are taken from THE MESSAGE, copyright © 1993, 2002, 2018 by Eugene H. Peterson. Used by permission of NavPress, represented by Tyndale House Publishers. All rights reserved.

Scripture quotations marked NIV are taken from the Holy Bible, New International Version®, NIV®. Copyright © 1973, 1978, 1984, 2011 by Biblica, Inc.™ Used by permission of Zondervan. All rights reserved worldwide. www.zondervan.com The "NIV" and "New International Version" are trademarks registered in the United States Patent and Trademark Office by Biblica, Inc.™

Scripture quotations marked KJV are from the King James Version of the Bible.

Copyright © 2024
By Richard Roberts
Tulsa, Oklahoma

ISBN 979-8-9883773-8-2

Published by Oral Roberts Evangelistic Association,

DBA Richard Roberts Ministries

PO Box 2187 • Tulsa, OK 74102-2187

All rights reserved.

Printed in the United States of America

TABLE OF CONTENTS

Introduction: Who Are You Trusting?

Chapter 1: Making God Your Source 11

Chapter 2: Biblical Stories of God's Provision 19

Chapter 3: Listening for God's Voice 29

Chapter 4: Trusting God by Faith 41

Chapter 5: Living with God as Your Source 51

Chapter 6: Source Questions and My Answers 55

Appendix: Scripture References and Declarations 61

Personal Notes

INTRODUCTION
Who Are You Trusting?

Are you struggling in your life right now? Do you need a financial miracle? Have you lost someone who used to be a provider? Have you lost your job? Has your stable life suddenly turned into what feels like quicksand? Have you ever wondered who the Source of your total supply really is?

Years ago, my father, Oral Roberts, had such a prophetic word from God about making Him our Source that I am compelled to pass on what I've learned from him to people today.

So, here is a portion of my dad's prophetic word because I think it's timely and powerful:

Oral Roberts: *The magnitude and the importance of His revelation for your life is like fire inside me, filling my being until I can hardly wait to COMMUNICATE it to you. The powerful anointing on this truth today is* like a fresh new wave over me. God's Word to His people is that we must MAKE GOD OUR SOURCE. God's people are not to live in poverty physically, spiritually, or financially. One of the tactics of the devil is to try to cut God's people off from their Source. Without that divine, miraculous supply from God as their Source, His people can be robbed of their faith, their hope, and things necessary to live life as God intended. God has already provided everything we need for our lives, and He is serious about having our needs met. We must learn the biblical way to get our needs met, and that is by faith in God our Source. God wanted us to realize that the just shall live by faith so much that He put it in His Word in four places: Habakkuk 2:4, Romans 1:17, Galatians 3:11, and Hebrews 10:38.

It all comes down to one question. Are you ready to turn to God as the Source of your total life-giving supply? I pray that you will reach up to Heaven with your faith and touch God, who is a good God and the Source of everything good for your life. Hear these words with the very EARS OF YOUR HEART AND SOUL – don't just read them as idle lines on paper. 2 Chronicles 20:20 says, "Believe in the Lord your God, so shall you be established; believe his prophets, so shall you prosper."

I have no doubt in my heart that God speaks to me in the spirit of a prophet, and when He speaks and I obey, His miracles happen. God has spoken to me again about making Him the Source of our total supply. I believe as we obey God we will be established, *and as we believe His prophets we will prosper and miracles will be our portion, in Jesus' Name!*

I pray for you to MAKE GOD YOUR SOURCE. Make Him your PHYSICAL SOURCE. Make Him your FINANCIAL SOURCE. And, above ALL, Make Him your SPIRITUAL SOURCE. THE SOURCE OF YOUR TOTAL SUPPLY.

When the Apostle Paul said in Philippians 4:19, "But my God shall supply ALL YOUR NEEDS according to his riches in glory by Christ Jesus," He meant ALL. This means that God can supply enough to meet all your needs when you make Him THE SOURCE OF YOUR TOTAL SUPPLY.

Life often presents us with difficult circumstances, and during these times, who we trust really matters. I've faced many such moments, and I've learned that trusting God as the Source of everything is not just comforting; it can be transformative.

One profound experience was when my wife, Lindsay, was diagnosed with stage 4 thyroid cancer. When Lindsay got the word, immediately her knees buckled, and she literally crumpled. But my girls and I surrounded her in that moment of fear and shut down that spirit with faith. We faced a mountain that at first seemed insurmountable. We declared healing over Lindsay, using the promises God gives us in the Bible.

I remember going out and picking up a little yellow rubber duck bath toy. I came back and gave it to her and said, "Lindsay, you are not a sitting duck waiting for the other shoe to drop. You are the righteousness of God in Christ Jesus, and you will overcome this." Lindsay held that duck every single day to remind herself that her faith had to be strong enough to push out the fear. After surgery we received a glorious report and today Lindsay is completely cancer-free, a testament to the power of God as our Source.

Sometimes, people find it hard to trust God, especially when things don't go as planned. They feel let down and might even blame God. But it's important to remember that we are not fighting against God. We're up against a real enemy who wants to steal, kill, and destroy (John 10:10). Understanding this can help us keep our trust in God and live out His promise of an abundant life.

Proverbs 3:5-6 NIV says, "Trust in the Lord with all your heart and lean not on your own understanding; in all your ways submit to him, and he will make your paths straight." This verse has guided me through many difficult times. To me, trusting God completely means seeking His guidance in every aspect of our lives.

We also need to understand that while we live in this world, we're not of it. (See John 15:19 & John 17:14-16.) You are of God, little children (1 John

4:4). Everything here on earth is described in 2 Corinthians 4:18 as temporary, including our problems. God, on the other hand, is our eternal Source. When everything else fails, the Bible says He remains steadfast.

As we navigate life's challenges, we have the opportunity to choose to lean not on our understanding, but on our faith in God.

CHAPTER 1

Making God Your Source

Oral Roberts: *Everything in life has a source. For example, every mighty river has a source. Perhaps at first, it's only a little spring way up in the mountains or a tiny stream of melted snow trickling down from the highest peaks. Then it becomes a little creek, then a river, until finally, the waters begin to flow toward the sea.*

I believe what the Apostle Paul declared in Acts 17:28: "In Him (Jesus) we live, and move, and have our being." God is the first and the last, the Alpha and the Omega, the beginning and the end (Revelation1:8). When the Lord gave Moses the Ten Commandments, He said, "Thou shalt have no other gods before me" (Exodus 20:3 KJV).

This means we must never let anything or anyone come between us and God, our Source. After all, doesn't everything come from God? Isn't He the Way, the Truth, and the Life (John 14:6)?

I believe some of the most important questions in life are these: Who is your Source? Who is your Supplier, who is your Savior, who is your Healer, who is your Deliverer? People may fail you. Businesses may fail. Governments may fail. But God never fails. His mercies are new every morning!

The Source of the Nile

If you turn off the source, how can the provision reach its destination? I'll never forget an experience I had which really proved to me the awesome power of God as the Source. It took place several years ago when I visited the headwaters of the Nile River in the African nation of Uganda. I was invited by the President of Uganda, Mr. Yoweri Museveni, to visit his country and conduct a healing crusade.

Each day, thousands came to a large soccer stadium to hear the preaching of the Word and receive prayer for the sick. My sponsor for the crusade was the Honorable Balaki Kirya, who was the Minister of State at that time. Mr. Kirya said to me, "Mr. Roberts, I'd like to take you to the source of the Nile River." Now, the Nile River flows out of Lake Victoria, which is about forty miles from Kampala, the capital city of Uganda. Also, the Nile is the only river in the world which flows from south to north.

As we stood at the place where the great Nile River begin its flow, he asked me a very sobering question. "Mr. Roberts, what do you think would happen if someone turned off the Nile River?" In a flash of a second, I realized that there are hundreds of villages, towns, and cities along the banks of the Nile, which flows through Central Africa, through the desert, and all the way up to the Mediterranean Sea. The Nile River sustains the millions upon millions of people who live along its banks. So, I replied, "If the river dried up, all the communities along its banks would dry up. And countless tens of thousands, perhaps millions of people would die.

I began to see in the Nile a tangible illustration of what God was saying to my dad about the importance of making God our Source…the Source of our total supply. While so many things we have previously depended on have changed or even completely dried up, God hasn't changed. Malachi 3:6 KJV says, *I am the Lord, I change not.* Hebrews 13:8 says, *Jesus Christ is the same yesterday, today and forever.* Philippians 4:19 KJV says, *But my God shall supply all your need according to his riches in glory by Christ Jesus.* And that has not changed.

The Provider Versus The Source

Understanding the difference between a provider and the source is crucial. Providers, like people, can come and go. They can offer support, but they are not always reliable. God, however, is our everlasting Source. He never changes, and His resources never run out. This is a comforting truth, especially when we face loss or change.

Philippians 4:19 KJV says, "But my God shall supply all your need according to his riches in glory by Christ Jesus." This verse reassures us that God's provision is not limited by our circumstances. He has limitless resources and can meet all our needs, whether they are physical, emotional, financial, or spiritual.

Making God your Source means your expectation is from Him.

The Bible says in Proverbs 3:5 "Trust in the Lord with all your heart, and lean not on your own understanding…" That is what He wanted the Israelites to do—to look only to Him to meet their needs. And that's what He wants us to do, too. He wants us to look to Him as the Source of all our needs. He WANTS to bless us! He WANTS to open the windows of heaven and pour out enormous blessings on His children. He wants every single need we have to be met!

God desires for us to make Him our ultimate Source of provision and blessing. Just as He led the

Israelites out of Egypt and into the wilderness to teach them to rely solely on Him, He wants us to move from looking to worldly sources to seeking His divine provision. When we trust in the Lord with all our hearts and lean not on our own understanding, we open ourselves up to receiving His abundant blessings.

I believe that no matter what challenges we may be facing, no matter how impossible the situation may seem, God is always by our side, ready to guide us and support us. He wants to pour out blessings upon us, to meet our every need and exceed our expectations. As we fix our eyes on Him, we can know that He is capable of meeting all our needs and desires. By making God our Source, we invite His divine favor and abundance into our lives, ready to receive the overflowing blessings He has in store for us. As you trust in the Lord, He is faithful to provide for all who seek Him.

The Taproot

I've heard my dad talk so much about "the taproot." A taproot is the large central root from which additional roots sprout. Every tree has a root system. It has hundreds of little roots, but the main source of its root system is the taproot. As long as the taproot is anchored in the soil and receives water, it will sustain the tree and the tree will bear much fruit.

It was this analogy that opened up my eyes to the truth of God as my Source. This is the same in life. If your root system is in God—if your taproot is anchored in Him—His Word says you can make it.

You may have made many other things your taproot in place of God as the main source of your supply. Perhaps you have made someone or something else your source. Perhaps your source is rooted in your spouse, your children, your parents, your church, your friends, your thinking, your emotions, your job, your bank account, or someone or something else. These may be good and necessary to you, but according to the Bible, God didn't intend for them to be the source of your life.

One or more "roots" in your life may change or be cut off, but if your inner man is anchored in the Lord, allowing God to be the taproot in your life, then you can continue to stand firm in the storms and tremors of life. If God is your center point, your Source, you can continue to live and be productive, filled with the joy of the Lord, no matter what comes your way. Of course, God can use people and circumstances as instruments to help us, but, ultimately, He is our Source.

In the eleventh chapter of Mark, I am reminded of the story of the fig tree Jesus cursed. The next day, the disciples seemed shocked that what Jesus spoke actually came to pass. One of the interesting things I noticed about this story is that Jesus, the miracle worker, had been around the disciples for quite some time and had taught them the value of speaking words and seeing how powerful they are. Jesus said that He did the things His Father sent Him to do, and part of that was teaching us the importance of speaking to our metaphoric mountains of difficulty, commanding them to be cast into the sea, not doubting in our heart, but believing the things that we say (according to God's will) would come to pass so that we would have what we say.

The take away I received from this is the fact that the tree dried up from the root…the source of its supply of nourishment. The moment Jesus cursed the fig tree, the rest of the tree began to dry up. Now, I understand that it took some time, but it was required to obey the Word of the Lord spoken by Jesus. God created this earth into existence by speaking His Word and set it up to respond whenever His Word and will went forth.

I believe Jesus was teaching His disciples and also teaching us a divine principle that rings true today and follows the pattern of making God our Source. When something like the fig tree is completely cut off from its source, it has no choice but to dry up. If we make something other than God our source, then there is the possibility of that thing or person or situation drying up. But, when we make God our Source, we discover that He is incapable of drying up. Therefore, we have a Source that will never leave us or forsake us, and a Source that we can count on for miracles every day of our lives.

James 1:17 NIV reminds us, "Every good and perfect gift is from above, coming down from the Father of the heavenly lights, who does not change like shifting shadows." This verse emphasizes that all good things come from God, reinforcing the idea that He is our consistent Source.

Today, when jobs are lost or someone's health is failing, or things can seem so uncertain, it's easy to feel like everything is falling apart. But as Christians, it is most important to know we can make sure God is our Source.

Shifting our trust from unstable systems to relying on God as our Source starts with a decision. Each day, we can choose to trust God and align our lives with His Word to get His promised outcome. Speaking positively and standing on God's promises are not just good habits; they are acts of faith that can activate God's power in our lives.

In every season of our lives, we can choose to see God as our Source. Whether we're facing financial difficulties, health issues, personal losses or something similar, God's supply remains constant. By turning to Him, we can find not only temporary relief, but everlasting support.

CHAPTER 2

Biblical Stories of God's Provision

The Bible is filled with stories that highlight God's provision and remind us of His faithfulness. These narratives offer valuable lessons and encourage us to trust in God's unchanging nature.

Peter's Miraculous Catch of Fish

In Luke 5, we read about Peter's miraculous catch of fish. But, it didn't start out that way.

After a hard night of fishing, Peter was sitting on the shore of the Sea of Galilee washing and mending his nets when, all of a sudden, a man came walking up to him. It was Jesus, and He needed a place to speak from to teach the people.

He took one look at Peter, and perhaps saw his empty fishing boat and said to him "… Lend me your boat."

Surely there must have been a conversation. In my imagination, I hear Peter saying something like, "… What do you need my boat for?" And Jesus replying, "I need it to preach from. Will you let me use it?"

So, Peter loaned his boat to Jesus, and Jesus preached and taught the people and most likely did miracles.

When He finished, He turned back to Peter and said to him "… Now, launch out into the deep waters and let down your nets for a catch."

I can imagine another conversation that might have followed. "Sir you don't look like a fisherman. You don't know how we fish in these waters. First of all, we don't fish during the day. We fish at night because the water in this lake is so clear that if we throw out the net during the day, the fish will see it and swim the other way. So, we fish at night. And we don't go out into the deep water, because it's too dangerous. Our boats are not strong enough to handle the storms that often come on these waters, so we fish only in the shallow water."

Jesus, however, wanted Peter to launch out into the deep waters where the big fish were. He was teaching Peter that God was his Source and not Peter's fishing techniques.

Peter talked with Him, saying, "... we have toiled all the night, and have taken nothing; nevertheless at thy word I will let down the net."

Notice that Jesus had said, ... Let down your '*nets*' for a catch. But Peter said, "... I will let down the '*net*' (Luke 5:5 KJV)."

Perhaps Peter had already washed and mended all of his nets except just one. Perhaps it was not his best net. Maybe it was an old one. It seems to me that Peter might not have believed the idea that God, who created the fish, could cause the fish to hit Peter's net. But he was about to find out.

As Peter prepared to launch his boat into the lake, Jesus stepped into the boat with him. And as they got into the deep waters, Peter threw out the net. Suddenly, perhaps much to Peter's surprise, fish began to fill the net. I can imagine the look on Peter's face as he began to haul in the fish and realize what was happening. It was a miracle!

As his boat was filling up with fish, Peter's net suddenly broke from the enormous weight of them all. I can imagine it was about that time when he wished he had brought extra nets with him. There were so many fish that Peter called on his fishing partners, who were in their own boats watching the scene unfold, to come and help gather the fish.

The Bible says they came over and their nets were filled as well. It was what my dad would call a "net-breaking, boat-sinking load of miracles." It makes me wonder what could have happened if Peter had fully trusted God and thrown out *all* his nets instead of just the one.

Peter saw the miracle right before his eyes. And there in his boat he got down on his knees and told Jesus to depart from him because he was a sinner. But Jesus told Peter no. He told him to get up and He would make something of Peter's life.

Peter was just beginning to learn that his fishing business was not his source. God was his Source.

The story of Peter's miraculous catch of fish serves as a poignant reminder, not only to Peter but to all who hear it, of God's boundless provision that often unfolds in unexpected ways, if we are willing to listen and obey.

The Widow's Oil

The story of the widow's oil in 2 Kings chapter 4, is another powerful example of how God can multiply what little we have. The widow was in a desperate situation. Her husband, who had been a powerful man of God and had helped support many prophets, had died. That was bad enough, but he had also left her in debt, and she had no way of paying it off.

When she received word that the creditors were coming to take her two sons as slaves in payment for the debt, she panicked, not knowing what to do. So, she turned to the Prophet Elisha for help.

Elisha, upon encountering the widow in her moment of distress, did not respond by offering her money or seeking to negotiate with her debtors. Instead, he approached the situation with a different perspective, asking the widow if she had anything of value in her possession. All she had was a small jar of oil. Elisha instructed her to send her two sons throughout the neighborhood and borrow as many vessels as possible, then bring them into the house and shut the door. Apparently, Elisha knew something about The Source that she did not.

How were these empty vessels and a small jar of oil going to solve her problem? It would take a miracle, and that is exactly what took place.

Elisha told the widow to begin to pour oil out of her one jar into the many empty vessels. Each time she filled a vessel, there was plenty left over to fill another, until they had filled every vessel the two sons had borrowed.

Elisha then told her to sell the oil she had collected, pay her debts and live on the remainder. By directing her focus towards what she already had, Elisha was leading her into a deeper understanding of God's ability to multiply even the smallest of resources into an abundance beyond measure. Through her obedience to Elisha's instructions, she saw a miraculous multiplication of that oil, a tangible manifestation of God's provision and faithfulness in her life.

The point is…she used what she had. Some people today do not understand this principle and do not use what they already possess. The widow finally realized that in her case, the miracle she needed was already in her house when she trusted God as her Source.

Psalm 37:25 NIV says, "I was young and now I am old, yet I have never seen the righteous forsaken or their children begging bread." This verse reassures us that God takes care of the righteous (those in right relationship with Him, in a partnership of faith). Even in the most challenging times, God's provision is evident.

The widow's story shows us that little can become something bigger when God is in it. Starting with limited resources, when we trust God and act in faith, He can multiply what we have to meet our needs and more.

Jehoshaphat's Victory

The story of Jehoshaphat in 2 Chronicles 20 is a testament to overcoming impossible odds by trusting in God. King Jehoshaphat faced three armies coming against him and the people of Israel. Instead of panicking, he fell on his face and began to pray and seek the Lord's direction. Then God sent the Prophet Jahaziel to tell the king and the people not to fear, that the battle was not theirs but God's. The Lord instructed Jehoshaphat to send his army to face the enemy and to put the praise and worship singers in front of the soldiers.

This was unusual and risky for these particular singers, as it meant they would advance on an enemy, but boldly the king obeyed the word of the Lord through the Prophet Jahaziel.

Because of the king's obedience to the word of the Lord, the enemy army turned on one another, destroying one another, and Israel won the battle without lifting a finger. The battle had been won without casualty on their part, and all that Jehoshaphat and the people of God had to do was to pick up the spoils that the enemy had left behind. There was so much that it took three days to gather all of the spoils. What a victory! They knew that God Almighty was their Source.

This story reminds us that no matter how overwhelming our circumstances might seem, God can intervene in miraculous ways. We may face challenges that seem insurmountable, but by trusting in God through our obedience and praising Him even in tough times, we can see amazing victories.

Like Jehoshaphat, we can also overcome impossible situations by putting our trust in God. When we face challenges that seem insurmountable, we can seek God in prayer and worship, knowing that He is able to do far more than we can imagine. By surrendering our fears and worries to Him, He can bring about miraculous outcomes.

Elijah and the Widow of Zarephath

In 1 Kings 17, God instructed the prophet Elijah to go to Zarephath during a severe famine. The Lord told him that he would meet a widow there who would sustain him.

When he arrived in town and met the woman, she was preparing food. He asked her for something to eat, and she told him that all she had was a little meal in a barrel and a little oil in a cruse. She was cooking one last dinner for herself and her son, and then they were going to die.

In verses 13-14, Elijah said to the woman, "Go ahead and cook your last supper, but give the first portion to me, for thus saith the Lord, if you'll do as I say, the meal in your barrel and the oil in your cruse shall not be diminished."

The widow obeyed the Word of the Lord. She finished cooking the meal and gave the first portion to the prophet of God. And miraculously, the next time she and her son were hungry, there was enough to cook again. And the next time they were hungry, once again, there was enough. Day after day and month after month, there was enough.

She and her son were sustained until the rains came and the drought was broken and they could plant their crops again. She learned that if she listened to the Lord and made Him the Source of her life, that she would be sustained. And she was.

The story of the widow of Zarephath teaches us the power of faith and obedience in the face of adversity. Despite being in the midst of a severe famine and facing the prospect of death, the widow trusted in the Word of the Lord delivered by the prophet Elijah. Through her obedience and willingness to put her faith in God, she experienced a miraculous provision that sustained her and her son through difficult times.

This story serves as a reminder that when we trust in God and follow His guidance, He will provide for our needs and sustain us through even the most challenging circumstances. Just as the widow's faith was rewarded with abundance and sustenance, we can find hope and strength in the Lord's promises, knowing that He will never abandon us in our time of need.

CHAPTER 3

Listening for God's Voice

To experience God's provision, we can cultivate a heart of expectancy. This means being open to the ways God can provide for us, even when they are unusual or unexpected. One way to do this is through prayer and reading the Bible. The more we immerse ourselves in God's Word, the more we understand His promises and learn to expect His provision.

Almost every morning, I start my day at 4:00 a.m. with prayer. I thank God for His provision in my life and declare His promises over my family, my ministry, and myself. This sets a positive tone for the day and helps me remain expectant of God's goodness.

Our words have power. Proverbs 18:21 tells us that "the tongue has the power of life and death." What we speak can shape our reality. When we speak words of faith, we align ourselves with God's promises and invite His power into our lives.

Hebrews 11:1 NIV says, "Now faith is confidence in what we hope for and assurance about what we do not see." This scripture reminds us that faith is about trusting in God's promises even when we cannot see the outcome. It's about having confidence in God's faithfulness.

Mark 11:24 NIV says, "Therefore I tell you, whatever you ask for in prayer, believe that you have received it, and it will be yours." This verse emphasizes the importance of belief in prayer. When we pray, according to God's will, we must believe that God hears us and that He is able to provide for our needs.

It's also important to be honest with God about our doubts and struggles. God is not offended by our questions; He invites us to bring our concerns to Him. Honest communication with God can deepen our faith and trust in Him. Being open with God about my fears and doubts brings me comfort and clarity. It's in these moments of honesty that I've felt God's presence most strongly, guiding me through difficult times.

James 1:5 NIV says, "If any of you lacks wisdom, you should ask God, who gives generously to all without finding fault, and it will be given to you."

Seeking God's wisdom in our decisions, whether big or small, allows us the opportunity to be aligned with His will and can open the door for His provision.

After periods of loss or change, God can lead us into new beginnings by staying open to His direction. For me, that requires faith and a willingness to let go of certain things from the past. I have found that there have been many times in my life when embracing new directions can lead to greater blessings and growth. Trusting God with my future means believing that He can bring something good out of every situation I face.

Many people I've encountered have always been fascinated by the idea of hearing the voice of God. In the Bible, Abraham heard the voice of God telling him to leave his own country and go to a place that God would show him (Genesis 12:1). Joshua heard the voice of God telling him to lead His people into the Promised Land (Joshua 1:2,3). Gideon heard the voice of God through an angel, calling him "a mighty man of valor" (Judges 6:11,12). When he was a child, Samuel heard the voice of God calling his name (I Samuel 3:10). Mary, the mother of Jesus, heard the voice of God through an angel, telling her that she was going to give birth to the Son of God (Luke 1:31). John heard the voice of God like the sound of a trumpet, saying, "I am the Alpha and the Omega, the First and the Last" (Revelation 1:10,11).

God is not limited in how He can speak to us.

And if He spoke to the people that I've just told you about, then He can still speak to men and women today. Why do I say that? Because Hebrews 13:8 says *He's the same yesterday, today, and forever!*

Three ways YOU can hear the voice of God

1. You can hear the still, small voice of God speaking in your spirit.

In I Kings 19, Elijah was being hunted down by Queen Jezebel, the wicked queen of Israel. She had put a bounty on his head, and she was going to have him executed. Elijah desperately needed to hear the voice of God, as he was looking for answers on how he could get away from Queen Jezebel.

Now Elijah was expecting to hear from God in some big, dramatic way to save him from this life or death issue. Let me tell you, God gave him some pretty dramatic special effects all right, but the answer didn't come in the way Elijah was expecting.

First, a great and powerful wind came roaring by, but the Lord wasn't in the wind. Then an earthquake shook the ground under his feet, but God wasn't in the earthquake. Next there was a roaring fire, but God wasn't in the fire either. Then Elijah heard a little, quiet voice speaking in his spirit. It was God speaking to him, telling him which way to go. It didn't happen exactly the way Elijah thought it would, but he heard the voice of God.

As you seek God for answers in your own life, I encourage you to look for the still, small voice of God, because while He can use grand gestures and miraculous signs, sometimes the perfect answer is a quiet word that meets your need.

How I heard the still, small voice of God

I remember some years ago when I heard the still, small voice of God speaking to me in the middle of an earthquake. Lindsay, our three daughters, and I, were asleep in a hotel room in California when the room began to shake violently. It was an earthquake that measured about 7.4 on the Richter scale. I had never experienced such a strong earthquake before, and, all at once, I realized how quickly my whole family could be swept away from me.

I began to pray and speak peace into the situation. It felt like everything could come toppling in on us and I knew that the only sustaining source of strength that I could lean on in that moment was God. As I made God the Source of total supply, I had no idea that I would need Him in the middle of an earthquake. But there, God was prepared to save us and keep us in His care regardless of what was shaking around us. During the chaos of the earthquake, I heard the quiet voice of God saying that He was there with me and that everything was going to be okay. As quickly as it started, the shaking stopped, the hotel didn't cave in around us, and I learned an important lesson from the Lord—He is the Source of my total supply.

When you make God the Source of your total supply, even a supply you didn't know you needed, you can hear the voice of God speaking quietly in your spirit, even when everything around you seems to be shaking.

2. You can hear the voice of God through a dream or a vision.

Acts 2:17 says that your young men shall see visions, and your old men shall dream dreams. In Genesis 37, God spoke to a young man named Joseph through a dream. Actually, the Lord gave him two dreams, and both of them revealed God's plan for his future. In the dreams, God used symbols to tell Joseph that someday his brothers, his mother, and even his father, were going to bow down to him, much to the dislike and scoffing from his family.

Joseph learned the hard way that sometimes it's better to keep a Word from the Lord to yourself rather than telling everybody else what God has said to you.

When his brothers heard about his dreams, they were furious. They sold him into slavery, and Joseph was brought to Egypt. It began to look like Joseph's days of dreaming were over, and his future would be full of nightmares. But God had different plans.

You might be thinking that if Joseph would have kept his mouth shut then none of this would have happened, but if Joseph hadn't told his brothers about his dreams, he might not have wound up in Egypt at all. And that's where he needed to be if God was going to use him and fulfill the dreams of Joseph's youth.

That tells me that God can even use our mistakes to get us into the position He needs us to be in so our dreams can be fulfilled. So, I say don't grieve over your mistakes. Give them to God. When we make God the Source of our total supply, He can turn mistakes and mishaps into miracles.

God is still speaking to us today through dreams and visions. What dreams and visions has God placed in your life? Does it feel like things are going wrong and you will never be able to fulfill them? Just like Joseph, sometimes our dreams take time, maturing, and positioning to come to fruition in our lives. I encourage you to stay steadfast, give your dreams and hopes to God, and allow Him to bring them to pass in His timing. Stay open to hearing from the Lord through your dreams and pray for understanding and discernment in walking them out.

3. You can hear the voice of God through His Word.

I believe one of the most important ways we can hear God's voice is through His Word. Are you asking yourself how you can know if this is really God speaking to you? If so, you can pick up your Bible and begin to read His Word. You see, God talks like He writes and He writes like He talks. His voice and His written Word will always line up.

I like to talk about God's Word as a guidebook for our life with the story of the disciples on the water.

One day the disciples were getting ready to take a boat ride, and Jesus told them, "Let us go over to the other side [of the lake]" (Mark 4:35 AMP).

Apparently, they didn't hear Him, or they forgot what He said, or they didn't really believe Jesus in the first place. Why do I say that? When they got into turbulence out in the middle of the lake, they panicked! I believe it was an attack of the devil. As soon as the trouble struck, they forgot all about what God had said to them through the words of Jesus. They forgot that the Lord had told them, "We're going over to the other side." And isn't that the way it happens sometimes?

Trouble strikes, and we forget what God said to us in His Word. We've heard the voice of God saying to us, in essence, "You're not going under. You're going over!" But, because of what's going on in the natural, it sometimes feels like there's no answer. However, the wonderful thing is when we make God our Source, we can tap into His Word and tap into what He said to us. His Word is designed to succeed, not fail.

When you face times of trouble, I encourage you to go to God's Word. Let it anchor you and look to it for advice. The Word of God is our greatest resource into knowing our Creator—what He says, thinks, and does. Make it your "go to" when you are looking for answers from God!

Two Habits You Can Develop

1. Be Obedient to God's Will

In Joshua 1, a young man named Joshua heard the voice of God. The Lord called him to lead the children of Israel into the Promised Land.

Was there anything special Joshua did to help him hear God's voice? I believe one of the most important things he did was to believe what God said.

In Numbers 13, Moses sent Joshua and 11 other men out on a spy mission to check out the Promised Land. Now they had already heard God's voice telling them that the land was theirs. But when they saw a few giants - a few roadblocks, a few obstacles - 10 of the spies started saying that there was no way they could take the land. But God had already said they could take the land. And Joshua and Caleb decided to agree with what God said. They stood up for God's Word, and they were the only ones out of the whole group who got to enter the Promised Land. I believe that standing up in obedience to God's plan also helped Joshua hear God's voice.

Another story of someone who was obedient to God's Word, even when the circumstances looked impossible, was Noah. Can you imagine how Noah must have felt when he heard the voice of God, warning him that there was going to be a great flood (Genesis 6)? Then the Lord told Noah to build a big ark so he and his whole family could escape from the floodwaters. Noah must have wondered what his neighbors were going to think when he started building the ark in his yard. But he obeyed God anyway.

Noah had decided to live for God in a world where nobody else seemed to care about the Lord. The people in his day probably thought he was crazy because he had taken such a strong stand for God. But while they were all out doing something else, Noah heard the voice of the Lord. He prepared himself for what was coming on the earth. And he and his whole household, plus two of each of the animals on the earth at that time, were the only ones who were saved from the flood.

To hear God's voice, I believe we, like Noah, have to decide to live for God, no matter what. It's like what the old gospel song says, "I have decided to follow Jesus... No turning back... No turning back..."

2. Develop A Consistent Prayer Life

To me, a consistent prayer life is regularly talking to God from your heart in the way that you would talk in your everyday life. It's a conversation with God, trusting and believing that, when you talk to Him, He hears and understands. But, in addition, I believe that it is important for us to listen for His response back to us, because communication with God is conversational. It's not just making my requests known to Him (as important as that is), it's fellowshipping with Him as Abba, Father. It's not me giving God my laundry list of everything that I want Him to do for me. It's communicating with God, talking with God in a very personal way that creates relationship.

God might speak back to you through His still small voice in your heart, or through His Word (the Bible), through a dream or vision, or through someone else who is listening to His still small voice on your behalf.

For me, the most important thing is to make quality time for communication and conversation with God as my Father. Proverbs 18:24 says that the Lord is the friend who sticks closer than a brother.

CHAPTER 4

Trusting God by Faith

The Bible makes known that God cares about every aspect of our lives—physical, financial, spiritual, emotional, and relational. Trusting Him as our Source means believing that He can meet all our needs.

How do we connect our faith and our needs? It can be hard to feel like God is our Source in the demands and chaos of our world, but the Bible says that God is with us and we can look to His Word to find our strength.

Jeremiah 29:11 NIV says, "For I know the plans I have for you," declares the Lord, "plans to prosper you and not to harm you, plans to give you hope and a future." This scripture is a powerful reminder that God has a plan for each of us. His plans are for our good, to give us hope and a future.

Isaiah 41:10 NIV says, "So do not fear, for I am with you; do not be dismayed, for I am your God. I will strengthen you and help you; I will uphold you with my righteous right hand." This verse reassures us that God is with us in every situation. He strengthens us, helps us, and upholds us with His righteous hand.

We don't need to aimlessly hope that we can withstand the storms of life. We can hold firm in our faith, relying on God as our Source so that nothing we face can shatter us. If we fall, we can get back up because God is strengthening us. If we are in a battle, we don't have to worry because it is God's plan to prosper us and give us a future.

I don't want to be like the disciples in the middle of the water, fearful and giving up hope. Remember, like Elijah, sometimes our answers are quiet. But, sometimes they are loud. It's up to God, not us, to determine the volume.

A faithful day with God as our Source may look like praying for wisdom in our work, asking for healing in our bodies, seeking peace in our relationships, or trusting God with our finances. God's desire is to make us whole (John 5:14). His Word says He is interested in every detail of our lives.

Even if we face loss or something that seemingly

alters our future, God can bring us comfort and hope or even bring something new and different than what we had before.

Hebrews 10:35 KJV says, "Cast not away therefore your confidence, which hath great recompense of reward." This shows that God wants to bless us as we keep our confidence in Him as the Source of our total supply. Hebrews 11:6 says that God is a rewarder when we diligently seek Him.

Isaiah 43:18, 19a in the Message Bible says, "Be alert, be present. I'm about to do something brand-new. It's bursting out."

Living by Faith

I see living by faith as trusting God in every aspect of my life. It influences my decisions, actions, and attitudes. Faith is not just for Sundays; it's for every day.

Second Corinthians 5:7 NIV says, "For we live by faith, not by sight." This verse underscores what our Christian walk is about. We are called to trust in God's promises even when we cannot see the outcome. It is about believing in His faithfulness regardless of our circumstances.

Habakkuk 2:4 NIV says, "See, the enemy is puffed up; his desires are not upright—but the righteous person will live by his faithfulness." Habakkuk 2:4

MSG says, "Look at that man, bloated by self-importance – full of himself but soul-empty. But the person in right standing before God through loyal and steady believing is fully alive, really alive." This scripture emphasizes that the righteous live by faith. This is not self-righteous, it is about being in right relationship with God. And it's our faith in God that can sustain us through life's challenges.

Proverbs 3:5-6 tells us to trust in the Lord with all our heart and lean not on our own understanding. This means putting our complete trust in God as the Source of our total supply, even if we don't understand His ways.

Romans 4:17 talks about calling things that are not as though they are. This means speaking in faith, even when we don't see the results yet. It doesn't mean we are living in denial or acting like an ostrich with our head in the sand…denying the existence of a situation.

However, it does mean we can be looking at the facts of the situation while commanding them to line up with the truth of the Word of God. We are declaring God's Word, believing that what He says is true and will come to pass as He promised. When speaking in faith, as we align ourselves with God's will, we invite His power into our lives. By declaring God's promises over situations, we can see miraculous outcomes.

Faith is Believing You Can Get to Where You Want to Be

You may be asking, "Is that possible for me?" My answer is—absolutely, yes. To me, a miracle is God's divine way of making a way where there seems to be no way. One of the greatest examples in the Bible dealing with an impossible situation that ends with a miracle is found in Mark 5:25-34 KJV:

> *"And a certain woman, which had an issue of blood twelve years, and had suffered many things of many physicians, and had spent all that she had, and was nothing bettered, but rather grew worse, when she had heard of Jesus, came in the press behind, and touched his garment. For she said, if I may touch but his clothes, I shall be whole. And straightway the fountain of her blood was dried up; and she felt in her body that she was healed of that plague. Jesus, immediately knowing in himself that virtue had gone out of him, turned him about in the press, and said, Who touched my clothes? And his disciples said unto him, Thou seest the multitude thronging thee, and sayest thou, Who touched me? And he looked round about to see her that had done this thing. But the woman fearing and trembling, knowing what was done in her, came and fell down before him, and told him all the truth. And he said unto her, Daughter, thy faith hath made thee whole. Go in peace, and be whole of thy plague."*

When I say to you that I believe God has a way for you to get to where you want to be, I say this as a Bible principle because of Jesus Christ. Jesus said of Himself, "I am the way, the truth, and the life; no man cometh unto the Father, but by me" (John 14:6 KJV). The way I read the Bible is that we can get from where we are to where we want to be by making God our Source through His Son, Jesus Christ, as our Savior—because Jesus is the Way.

We Can Take the First Step

I believe that nothing would have ever happened until the woman with the issue of blood took the first step by acting on her faith. James 2:17 says that faith without works is as good as dead. Here, the word "works" means "corresponding action."

Jesus did His part through the action of going to the cross for our salvation and healing. He declared His job was finished because it was. Now, it's up to us to do our part and that is to believe God's Word by the action of our faith and expect a miracle, believing that God is the Source of our total supply.

Trusting God for Your Financial Supply

I remember a question my dad once asked when he said, "Have you ever stopped to think that the devil is stealing your money from you?" He was speaking to a large audience and suddenly you could sense a hush go over the room. People were genuinely pondering the answer to that question.

Then he followed it up with the scripture in John 10:10, which states that the thief, or the devil, comes to kill, steal, and destroy. But, Jesus said, "I have come that they may have life, and that they may have it more abundantly."

In my life, I've never found lack to be glorious. Psalms 24:1 KJV says the earth is the Lord's and the fullness thereof. Haggai 2:8 KJV declares that the silver is mine and the gold is mine, sayeth the Lord of hosts. In reading that, it tells me that the devil did not create nor does he own this earth. God created it and owns it.

Deuteronomy 8:18 says that it is the Lord that gives us power to get wealth. Psalm 35:27 says that God takes pleasure in the prosperity of His servants. Proverbs 10:22 says the blessing of the Lord makes one rich and adds no sorrow with it. It does not say that God blesses us with lack and suffering and without a way to figure out how to have our needs met.

Genesis 14:19, 20 KJV tells us that Abraham gave God tithes of all. The priest of God, Melchizedek, declared, "Blessed be Abram of the most high God, possessor of heaven and earth: And blessed be the most high God, which hath delivered thine enemies into thy hand. And he (Abraham) gave him tithes of all." As Abraham made God his Source and God began to bless him, there was no one like him on earth.

Malachi 3:10 KJV says, "Bring ye all the tithes into the storehouse…and prove me now herewith, saith the Lord of hosts, if I will not open you the windows of heaven and pour you out a blessing, that there shall not be room enough to receive it."

Philippians 4:19 declares my God shall provide all our needs according to His riches in glory by Christ Jesus. To me, that is blessed beyond measure.

God's Provision for Forgiveness

Ephesians 4:32 NIV says, "Be kind and compassionate to one another, forgiving each other, just as in Christ God forgave you."

Colossians 3:13-14 NIV says, "Bear with each other and forgive one another if any of you has a grievance against someone. Forgive as the Lord forgave you. And over all these virtues put on love, which binds them all together in perfect unity."

James 1:5 NIV says, "If any of you lacks wisdom, you should ask God, who gives generously to all without finding fault, and it will be given to you."

Matthew 18:21-22 NIV says, "Then Peter came to Jesus and asked, 'Lord, how many times shall I forgive my brother or sister who sins against me? Up to seven times?' Jesus answered, 'I tell you, not seven times, but seventy-seven times.'" This scripture emphasizes the importance of continual forgiveness. This does not approve of someone else's offense, it simply reminds us to forgive.

God's Provision for Relationships

Making God your Source in every area includes relationships. He wants to meet our every need (Philippians 4:19)—and that includes our relational needs. Here are some scriptures to consider when praying about this…

Proverbs 15:1 NIV says, "A gentle answer turns away wrath, but a harsh word stirs up anger."

Ephesians 5:33 NIV says "However, each one of you also must love his wife as he loves himself, and the wife must respect her husband."

James 1:19, 20 NKJV "So then, my beloved brethren, let every man be swift to hear, slow to speak, slow to wrath; for the wrath of man does not produce the righteousness of God."

1 Thessalonians 5:11 NKJV "Therefore comfort each other and edify one another, just as you also are doing."

Ecclesiastes 7:9 NKJV "Do not hasten in your spirit to be angry, For anger rests in the bosom of fools."

CHAPTER 5

Living with God As Your Source

Living with God as our Source can transform every aspect of our lives. God has the power to bring peace, provision, and purpose. We can trust God and believe that He can meet all our needs, no matter the circumstances.

Romans 8:28 NIV says, "And we know that in all things God works for the good of those who love him, who have been called according to his purpose." This verse reassures us that God is working for our good in every situation.

Jeremiah 29:11 NIV says, "For I know the plans I have for you," declares the Lord, "plans to prosper you and not to harm you, plans to give you hope and a future." We can trust that God has a purpose and a good plan for us and that plan gives us hope and a future.

Philippians 4:13 NIV says, "I can do all this through him who gives me strength." This scripture emphasizes that our strength comes from God.

As we live each day, we can remember that God is interested in the details of our lives, and that He cares about our physical health, financial stability, spiritual growth and relationships. We can trust Him as our Source, opening our hearts to His total provision.

Daily practices can help us stay connected to God as our Source. Starting each day with prayer, thanking God for His provision, and declaring His promises can set a godly tone for the day. Reading the Bible regularly can immerse us in God's Word, helping us understand His promises and build our faith.

Our words matter. We can invite God's power into our lives by declaring His promises. Being honest with God about our doubts and struggles can deepen our relationship with Him and help us trust Him more. Staying open to new beginnings and trusting that God can bring something good out of every situation, can lead us into new opportunities. (See Isaiah 43:19.)

**Three thoughts to meditate
on from the Word:**

1. God wants us to have abundant life. (John 10:10)

2. God wants us to prosper and be in health even as our soul prospers. (3 John 2)

3. As we delight ourselves in the Lord, God wants to give us the desires of our heart. (Psalm 37:4)

CHAPTER 6

Source Questions and My Answers

Q - What is the difference between source versus a provider?

A- The source is the ultimate provider, or as Oxford Dictionary says "the place from which something comes." A provider means bringing something for your use.

Think about a light switch. You flip the switch to provide light, but the power company is the actual source of that light. Similarly, a job or person might provide for your needs, but I believe God is the ultimate Source. Providers may be temporary and can change, but God is constant, and His resources are unlimited.

A provider could be someone at your job or business, someone bringing gifts, your boss, a teacher, etc. But the way I read the Bible, things or people are not your source. God created us to connect to Him as the ultimate Source of our supply.

Q - Why does it matter if God is the Source in real life?

A- Life is ever-changing—jobs, relationship, finances—but God never changes. When we make God our Source, we are connecting to an unlimited and reliable supply that never runs out.

Hebrews 11:1 NIV says, "Now faith is confidence in what we hope for and assurance about what we do not see." By having faith in God as our Source, we trust in His ability to provide for us even when we can't see the immediate solution. This helps us to stay steady and secure, believing that God's provision is always available and sufficient for our needs.

When we depend on God as our Source, we are not left to the uncertainties and failures of worldly providers. Instead, we can stand firm on the promise that God will supply all our needs according to His riches in glory by Christ Jesus (Philippians 4:19). This scripture allows us to live confidently and with hope, regardless of our circumstances.

Q - How do I live by this principle?

A - For me, it's prayer, studying God's Word, and

believing in God's promises. You get the right answers when you ask the right questions. God makes it simple in Matthew 7:7 which says, "Ask, and it will be given to you; seek, and you will find; knock, and it will be opened to you."

Begin to pray, believing God for His provision in your life. The Bible says you have to believe it and hold on to that belief. It's easy to feel hopeless when you're believing for something and nothing seems to happen. But Galatians 6:9 says not to be weary in our well-doing because we reap when we don't give up, when we refuse to quit. Consistent faith and persistence are vital!

Q - How do I pray and what do I say?

A - Prayer is talking to God from your heart. You don't have to use big fancy words. Talk to Him like you would talk to a close friend and allow Him to talk back to you. For example: "God, I need your help today. Thank you for being there for me and giving me strength. Amen." It's that simple.

Prayer is a two-way conversation between you and God. Some people are afraid to pray because they don't know how, because they don't think they can talk to God like He's their friend. But He is! He's on your side. Talk to Him like you're talking to an old friend.

Q - Do I really have anything to give?

A - When you think about things to give, many people tend to think you can only give out of your financial resources or out of some material resource, but God wants us to give as He instructs.

Moses parted the Red Sea with something he had in his hand. He had a shepherd's rod - a stick, for all practical purposes. When he decided to use the authority that he had from his Source, God used a stick in his hand to part the Red Sea. There's no way a stick could have parted the sea on its own, but he used what he had as God directed, and the anointing of God took over and did the rest.

When we do what God tells us to do in obedience, whether it's to give something material, or to mentor someone, or to change to a different job or position, or pray for someone, we connect ourselves to God as our Source and then He can provide the anointing to get the job done and get the needs met.

Q - As a new believer, how do I establish God as my Source?

A- Like anything in life, you must first choose. I believe choosing to have a personal relationship with God is step number one. I encourage you to get a Bible. Inside, you will find truths to show you that God loves you. He is trustworthy, dependable, and ready to meet your needs.

Be diligent in making a daily practice of reading your Bible. As you consistently read the Word of God, you can quickly see that it points you to Him as the Source of everything you need. Start with Matthew, Mark, Luke, John and the book of Acts. There you will see Jesus in His earthly life and ministry and understand why He came to give you abundant life.

In addition, please see the list of scriptures on the following pages that I have added for you to read, declare, and meditate on to help you establish God as your source.

I Want to Pray for You Right Now...

I pray for you to come to know God as the Source of your total supply. I ask the Lord to bless you in every area of your life,—spiritually, physically, financially, in your soul, in your relationships and in any way that you need His divine intervention. If you need Jesus, I pray that you will ask Him to forgive you of any sin, release any wrong-doing and that you accept Jesus as your Lord and Savior. I pray for God's highest and best blessings in your life as you make Him the Source of your total supply to meet your every need. In Jesus' name, Amen.

If you need further prayer, you can contact us at The Abundant Life Prayer Group at 918-495-7777 or www.richardroberts.org.

APPENDIX

Scripture References and Declarations

Daily Reminders

1. God is my provider, and I trust in His provision for all my needs. (*Philippians 4:19*)

2. God is my refuge and strength, a very present help in times of trouble. (*Psalm 46:1*)

3. God is my rock and my fortress, my deliverer in whom I take refuge. (*Psalm 18:2*)

4. God is my shepherd; I shall not want. (*Psalm 23:1*)

5. God is my light and my salvation, whom shall I fear? (*Psalm 27:1*)

6. God is my guide and my compass, leading me on the path of righteousness. (*Psalm 23:3*)

7. God is my strength and my shield, my heart trusts in Him, and I am helped. (*Psalm 28:7*)

8. God is my source of wisdom and understanding, guiding me in all my decisions. (*James 1:5*)

9. God is my healer, and by His wounds, I am healed. (*Isaiah 53:5*)

10. God is my source of peace, and His peace surpasses all understanding. (*Philippians 4:7*)

11. God is my source of joy, and His joy is my strength. (*Nehemiah 8:10*)

12. God is my source of courage, and I can be strong and courageous because He is with me. (*Joshua 1:9*)

13. God is my future and my hope. (*Jeremiah 29:11*)

14. God's love never fails. (*1 Corinthians 13:8*)

15. God's grace is sufficient for me. (*2 Corinthians 12:9*)

16. God will never leave me nor forsake me. (*Hebrews 13:5*)

17. God is my source of salvation, and in Him, I have eternal life. (*Hebrews 5:9*)

18. God is working miracles on my behalf. (*Job 5:9*)

19. God sent His angels to protect me. (*Psalm 91*)

20. God is my help in time of trouble. (*Psalm 46:1*)

My Declarations

1. I am fearfully and wonderfully made. (*Psalm 139:14*)

2. I can do all things through Christ who strengthens me. (*Philippians 4:13*)

3. I am more than a conqueror through Him who loved me. (*Romans 8:37*)

4. I am blessed and highly favored. (*Ephesians 1:3*)

5. I am a new creation in Christ. (*2 Corinthians 5:17*)

6. I am strong and courageous because the Lord is with me. (*Joshua 1:9*)

7. I choose to walk in love. (*1 John 4:7*)

8. I am an overcomer. (*Revelation 12:11*)

9. I am chosen and called by God for a purpose. (*2 Timothy 1:9*)

10. I am filled with the joy of the Lord, which is my strength. (*Nehemiah 8:10*)

11. I am secure in my identity as a child of God, chosen and loved by Him. (*1 Peter 2:9*)

12. I am a peacemaker. (*Matthew 5:9*)

13. I am blessed in every area of my life. (*Deuteronomy 28*)

14. I live in peace because my mind is stayed on Him and I trust Him. (*Isaiah 26:3*)

15. I am the righteousness of God in Christ Jesus. (*2 Corinthians 5:21*)

Scriptures to Meditate On:

3 John 2 NKJV

Beloved, I pray that you may prosper in all things and be in health, just as your soul prospers.

John 3:16 NKJV

For God so loved the world that He gave His only begotten Son, that whoever believes in Him should not perish, but have everlasting life.

Psalm 103:1-5 KJV

1 Bless the Lord O my soul: and all that is within me, bless his holy name.

2 Bless the Lord, O my soul, and forget not all his benefits:

3 Who forgiveth all thine iniquities; who healeth all thy diseases;

4 Who redeemeth thy life from destruction; who

crowneth thee with loving kindness, and tender mercies;

5 Who satisfieth thy mouth with good things; so that thy youth is renewed like the eagle's.

Matthew 6:9-13 KJV—The Lord's Prayer

9 Our Father which art in heaven, Hallowed be thy name.

10 Thy kingdom come, Thy will be done in earth, as it is in heaven.

11 Give us this day our daily bread.

12 And forgive us our debts, as we forgive our debtors.

13 And lead us not into temptation, but deliver us from evil: for thine is the kingdom, and the power, and the glory, for ever. Amen.

Safety when abiding in the presence of God:

Psalm 91 NKJV

1 He who dwells in the secret place of the Most High Shall abide under the shadow of the Almighty.

2 I will say of the Lord, "He is my refuge and my fortress; My God, in Him I will trust."

3 Surely He shall deliver you from the snare of the fowler And from the perilous pestilence.

4 He shall cover you with His feathers, And under His wings you shall take refuge; His truth shall be your shield and buckler.

5 You shall not be afraid of the terror by night, Nor of the arrow that flies by day,

6 Nor of the pestilence that walks in darkness, Nor of the destruction that lays waste at noonday.

7 A thousand may fall at your side, And ten thousand at your right hand; But it shall not come near you.

8 Only with your eyes shall you look, And see the reward of the wicked.

9 Because you have made the Lord, who is my refuge, Even the Most High, your dwelling place,

10 No evil shall befall you, Nor shall any plague come near your dwelling;

11 For He shall give His angels charge over you, To keep you in all your ways.

12 In their hands they shall bear you up, Lest you dash your foot against a stone.

13 You shall tread upon the lion and the cobra, The young lion and the serpent you shall trample underfoot.

14 "Because he has set his love upon Me, therefore I will deliver him; I will set him on high, because he has known My name.

15 He shall call upon Me, and I will answer him; I will be with him in trouble; I will deliver him and honor him.

16 With long life I will satisfy him, And show him My salvation."

Philippians 4:13-19 KJV

13 I can do all things through Christ which strengtheneth me.

14 Notwithstanding ye have well done, that ye did communicate with my affliction.

15 Now ye Philippians know also, that in the beginning of the gospel, when I departed from Macedonia, no church communicated with me as concerning giving and receiving, but ye only.

16 For even in Thessalonica ye sent once and again unto my necessity.

17 Not because I desire a gift: but I desire fruit that may abound to your account.

18 But I have all, and abound: I am full, having received of Epaphroditus the things which were sent from you, an odour of a sweet smell, a sacrifice acceptable, well pleasing to God.

19 But my God shall supply all your need according to his riches in glory by Christ Jesus.

Galatians 6:7-9 KJV

> *7 Be not deceived; God is not mocked: for whatsoever a man soweth, that shall he also reap.*

> *8 For he that soweth to his flesh shall of the flesh reap corruption; but he that soweth to the Spirit shall of the Spirit reap life everlasting.*

> *9 And let us not be weary in well doing: for in due season we shall reap, if we faint not.*

Ephesians 6:10-18 KJV

> *10 Finally, my brethren, be strong in the Lord, and in the power of his might.*

> *11 Put on the whole armour of God, that ye may be able to stand against the wiles of the devil.*

> *12 For we wrestle not against flesh and blood, but against principalities, against powers, against the rulers of the darkness of this world, against spiritual wickedness in high places.*

> *13 Wherefore take unto you the whole armour of God, that ye may be able to withstand in the evil day, and having done all, to stand.*

> *14 Stand therefore, having your loins girt about with truth, and having on the breastplate of righteousness;*

> *15 And your feet shod with the preparation of the gospel of peace;*

16 Above all, taking the shield of faith, wherewith ye shall be able to quench all the fiery darts of the wicked.

17 And take the helmet of salvation, and the sword of the Spirit, which is the word of God:

18 Praying always with all prayer and supplication in the Spirit, and watching thereunto with all perseverance and supplication for all saints.

Personal Declarations for Myself and My Family

My Takeaway Notes from this Book

RICHARD ROBERTS

Richard Roberts, B.A., M.A., D.Min., is the Chairman and CEO of Richard Roberts Ministries and has dedicated his life to ministering the saving, healing, delivering power of Jesus Christ around the world.

Richard has ministered God's healing power in 39 nations, spanning six continents. In his healing outreaches, Richard has ministered to crowds of over 200,000 people in a single service. His services are marked with supernatural miracles and healings by a tremendous move of the Spirit. Today, Richard focuses on his *Greater Works* International Pastor's Conferences where he teaches and trains pastors in underdeveloped nations.

Richard and his wife, Lindsay, also host *The Place for Miracles*—a half-hour inspirational TV broadcast that reaches out to millions worldwide. Together, Richard and Lindsay minister by the power of the Holy Spirit.

In 2010, Richard opened *The Richard Roberts*

School of Miracles, offering online Bible courses with practical, hands-on experience.

In 2023, Richard and Lindsay launched **The Healing Network**, a powerful 24-hour network for healing prayers and anointed messages.

Richard hosts a weekly podcast, *Expect a Miracle,* sharing teachings and conversations to inspire listeners to expect the miracles they need in life.

He has authored a number of publications and other inspirational material, including …*Your Road to a Better Life, Unstoppable Increase, He's A Healing Jesus, God's Healing Touch,* and *Thrive—Eliminating Lack from Your Life.*

If you need prayer, you can contact us at

The Abundant Life Prayer Group at

918-495-7777,

or online at

www.RichardRoberts.org

www.RichardRoberts.org